Cotswold
Architecture & Heritage

Cotswold

— Architecture & Heritage —

Photographs by F.A.H. Bloemendal
Text by Alan Hollingsworth

LONDON

IAN ALLAN LTD

Left:
St Mary's Fairford A superb example of a Cotswold 'wool church', St Mary's was almost completely rebuilt c1490-1500 by a local wool-merchant, John Tame. The work was continued after his death in 1500 by his son, Sir Edmund Tame. The numerous and very large windows with their tall mullions and rectilinear tracery, the battlemented parapet on the nave and chancel, and the pinnacled buttresses with the elaborately pierced parapet and double pinnacles of the tower are all indications of the richness of the late Perpendicular style. So too are the many carvings on the tower and along the string-course. The church is particularly famous for its painted glass which has survived frequent wars and innumerable vandals since it was completed early in the 16th century. The artist is believed to have been Bernard Flower who also worked on the glass in King's College Chapel, Cambridge. The 28 windows tell the Bible story from Adam and Eve through the Crucifixion and Resurrection to the Final Judgement and depict all the horrors the medieval mind could contrive. There are believed to be over 1,000 different figures. The quality and the sheer craftsmanship of churches like Fairford reflect the enormous skill of all those engaged in the task of building them over the centuries – from the genius of the master-masons' designs to the artistry of the humble carver of the choir stalls – corporate skill that in the early 16th century was nearing perfection and hence, inevitably perhaps, its own demise . . .

CONTENTS

Introduction 5
1 Oxfordshire 18
2 Warwickshire and Worcestershire 36
3 Gloucestershire ... 48
4 Avon and Wiltshire 68
Bibliography 95
Index 96

IAN ALLAN
DATE 08.11.90 TIME 09:45
JOB PP-1.rwo . 100

First published 1992

ISBN 0 7110 1960 6

Published by Ian Allan Ltd, Shepperton, Surrey; and printed by Ian Allan Printing Ltd at their works at Coombelands in Runnymede, England

Introduction

In the companion volume, *Cotswold Landscape*, we enjoyed a landscape artist's view of the broader vistas of the Cotswolds — its hills, its valleys and streams, its villages sparkling in the sunshine, its elegant stone-built towns. In this book we narrow down the focus and look rather more closely at the matchless heritage of Cotswold buildings in a variety of styles and periods, but all of them using the bedrock of the Cotswolds, its oolitic limestone most of which rejoices in the name of 'freestone'.

Opinions on the origin of that name vary. Some say that it is 'free' because neatly rectangular slabs suitable for the tight-jointed high quality building method we call 'ashlar' can be lifted straight out of the rock face. Others that because of its fine texture masons can cut it freely in any direction with a saw — and hence 'freemasons' (as distinct from 'rough' masons who build from uncut rubble). Either way or both, the ease with which Cotswold stone can be cut, carved and sculpted and the way in which it hardens after exposure to the weather has made it

Left:
Hailes Abbey, Winchcombe Until its destruction following the Dissolution of the Monasteries in 1539, Hailes Abbey comprised a massive range of buildings centred upon an abbey church even larger than that in Fairford and all built of local stone. Judging by the quality of fragments of masonry in the excellent English Heritage museum on the site, it was of the same superlative craftsmanship. A Cistercian establishment, it was founded in 1246 under the patronage of Richard, Earl of Cornwall, King of the Romans and a brother of Henry III. Following a vow made when his life was in serious danger at sea, he provided the new abbey with land and also with a phial said to contain the blood of Christ. Over the following centuries this made Hailes a centre of pilgrimage comparable with Canterbury and Walsingham. At the Dissolution the phial was found to contain 'honey clarified with saffron, as had been evidently proved before the King and his Council'. In 1542 the Crown sold the abbey to an agent who demolished the church and other buildings leaving the cloister and the abbot's lodging standing. In the 17th century they became converted into a house by the Tracy family and old prints show a gabled and mullioned house typical of the period – built no doubt by local masons with stone from the abbey. Later the house was demolished and the site became a stone quarry – the fate of many monastic buildings. Seen here is the eastern range of the cloister, its three central arches leading into what is left of the chapter house in the foreground. Hailes Abbey was given to the National Trust in 1937 and is open to the public under the control of English Heritage.

highly sought after since men first built in stone. The unmistakable Cotswold style of building evolved in the Middle Ages from the sheer workability of the local stone and has been copied all along the belt where similar stone can be found from South Dorset to South Lincolnshire. The stone itself is an oolitic limestone of the Jurassic period which means in effect that it was laid down between c135 and 185 million years ago. An authority on Cotswold stone was the late H. J. Massingham. He says that the limestone of the Cotswold region is among what he calls 'Thursday's Stones'. If, he argues, it took six days to create the Earth and today is the Sabbath when we are enjoying the fruits of creation, then the Jurassic period when the Cotswold stone was made would have been Thursday — geologically the day before yesterday — 'the day just before the humble were exalted and the little mammals stepped into the kingdom of the great saurians, the day that is called Jurassic'. Evidence of both those dinosaurs and the little mammals who succeeded them is frequently found in fossil form in Cotswold stone.

So much then for Cotswold stone and its origins which were covered in greater detail in *Cotswold Landscape*. In this volume our main interest is in the ways in which it is used and the manner in which the unique Cotswold building style evolved over the centuries.

As any mason, free or otherwise, will tell you, the masonic craft goes back into early biblical times when the elements of the style we call 'Classical' had their origins. In the Cotswolds it certainly goes back to about 2000BC when the ancients built their long barrows with shaped pillars of Great Oolite and used tilestone for the skilfully laid drystone walling in the portals of barrows like that at Belas Knap near Snowshill. The Romans also built in Cotswold stone using it first for building roads across the region. These include the great Fosse Way which runs along the limestone belt from Seaton on the Devon coast, through Bath and across the country to Lincoln; Ermine Street from London through Silchester to Gloucester and on into South Wales; and Akeman Street running northeastwards to St Albans. Where these arterial roads crossed they built their biggest civil development in the area, *Corinium Dubunorrum*, which we know as Cirencester. At the end of the 2nd century AD it covered an area of 250 acres, its forum and basilica were second in size only to those of London and both it and the surrounding countryside abounded with wealthy villas, many of them stone-built. The style of those civic buildings and of the town and country mansions were local variants of the 'Classical' style the Romans used throughout their vast empire: columns and pediments, rounded arches, mosaic floors, much decorative carving and sculpture. Except in a depraved 'Romanesque' form it disappeared from the cities of Europe with the end of the Roman Empire around 400AD and did not reappear in Italy until the Renaissance in the late 15th century or return to Britain until the 17th century, and to the Cotswolds in the 18th century.

It is often said that for enduring buildings three things are necessary: money, masons and stone. In the Cotswolds the stone, as we have seen, is always there. In Roman times there was also the money, much of it coming from the wool produced by the large flocks of sheep in the area. The long-standing Roman tradition of building in stone produced the masons. But by 500AD the Romans had long gone and so had the wealth and the masons. Their successors, that group of Germanic invaders we call Saxons, were by tradition builders in timber and growers of corn. In the Cotswolds they found timber plentiful and where the timber was cleared, land that grew corn well. But there was little surplus wealth and fewer masons. The onset of Christianity from the 7th century onwards led to quite extensive church and monastery building, but for the most part it was in timber and thatch even in areas where stone was readily available. Late in the Saxon period some abbeys and churches were built of stone in a very simple style employing large stones going right through the walls at the corners, alternatively standing vertically and horizontally, which we now call 'long and short' work. The Saxon style also included tiny round-headed window openings carved from single stones and distinctive pilaster strips as decoration. Most traces of Saxon churches in the Cotswolds area are found in odd stones and carvings incorporated into buildings of a later date but churches at Coln Rogers, Bradford-on-Avon and Duntisbourne Rouse are still largely Saxon in style.

The Norman lords and bishops who took over control of the country after 1066 brought with them a strong stone-building tradition based on the oolitic limestones of Normandy which are very similar to those of

Left:
St Lawrence, Bradford-on-Avon When it was completed about 1000AD, this little stone-built church would probably have been one of the very few stone buildings to have been built in the Cotswold area since Roman times. The stone is 'Superior' or 'Great' Oolite of the 'Bath' variety and is believed to have come from the quarry opened by St Aldhelm at Box to provide stone for his abbey at Malmesbury, c700AD. The provenance of the church itself is uncertain. It was lost for centuries among other buildings and was at one time used as two cottages. It was rediscovered in 1856 and restored, but historians since have disagreed about its origins. Some say it was built by St Aldhelm at the end of the 7th century; others that it was rebuilt by Ethelred the Unready, c1001 to protect the relics of St Edward the Martyr from the marauding Danes. The style is late Saxon as evidenced by its small size – the nave is only 25ft (8m) long – its steep and narrow proportions, the tiny round-headed doors and windows and the pilaster strips. One curious feature is its orientation – ENE instead of the more usual east.

the Cotswolds. (In the southeast of England they imported Caen stone for centuries. Parts of the Tower of London and Westminster Abbey are built of it.) And with them came the masons — master-masons who could both design and build; free-masons who could carve and mould; rough-masons who built the rubble walls. First they built the castles to hold the country in an iron grip. Then they built the cathedrals, the abbeys and the churches in stone to strengthen the hold of their Rome-based version of the Christian church and to oust the prevailing Celtic form, sweeping away and rebuilding the Saxon timber buildings as they did so. The century that followed the Conquest was one of enormous building achievement — some call it one of the wonders of the medieval age — all over the country. The money for most of this building came from the wool trade which grew steadily throughout the Norman period when England had a virtual monopoly. One advantage was the prevalence of low dry grassy hills suitable for grazing sheep and the other the almost complete absence of wolves. The Cotswolds had the finest sheep walks and in the large long-woolled Cotswold breed, the most productive sheep. They also had the Roman legacy of decent access roads.

There was extensive Norman building in the area both sacred and secular, but much has either disappeared or been incorporated into later buildings. There were several great abbeys: Augustinian at Cirencester, Benedictine at Gloucester, Tewkesbury, Winchcombe, Pershore, Evesham and Malmesbury, Cistercian at Hailes. Apart from one castle — at Beverstone — and a few domestic buildings, the main Norman heritage is of churches, and there are very few in the Cotswolds that do not show some trace of their Norman origins in the 'Romanesque' style: strong and simple, thick walls, small openings, massive columns, semi-circular arches, decoration confined to chevron mouldings and the carving of capitals of columns and of sculptured tympana over doors. Dragons' heads, grotesques of all kinds and especially beak heads are typical and recurrent Norman features.

By the end of the 12th century, this rounded Romanesque style was being replaced by the pointed arches of what we now call the 'Gothic' style. Its great advantage was that it allowed the master masons who were the architects of the day, to open up and literally to enlighten their churches in a manner previously impossible. Walls could be made thinner, windows bigger and columns lighter than in the earlier Norman style. Naturally this didn't happen suddenly or all at once and the Gothic style steadily evolved from its introduction at the start of the 12th century, until its gradual eclipse 300 years later. Historians have defined three main periods of this evolution when significant changes in stylistic detail occurred. The first, which we call 'Early English', covers the entire 13th century and is characterised by tall lancet windows in groups of three (to represent the Trinity) or five with thick vertical mullions. The second is the 'Decorated' style when the lancets had thinner mullions and were surmounted by complicated but delicate bar tracery — 'more tracery than glass' — a vogue which lasted from c1290 to c1350. The final period which lasted nearly 200 years is known as the 'Perpendicular' and is characterised by rectilinear panels of delicate tracery and 'more glass than tracery'; indeed, often by more glass than wall. The 'Perpendicular' made its first appearance c1350 in the Abbey Church in Gloucester (now Gloucester Cathedral) and represents the long and glorious flowering of the Gothic style in Britain. It is essentially English and not found outside present and former British realms. In England it is quintessentially a 'wool-church' style and in the wool-producing areas from the Cotswolds to East Anglia, from Somerset to Yorkshire there are very few churches that do not have some 'Perpendicular' feature.

In the Cotswolds during all this time not only was the stone always there, so too were the masons — and their essential counterparts, the carpenters. Both were itinerant bands of craftsmen employed under contract, sometimes for life, by the church hierarchy and monastic foundations. The term 'mason' embraced a range of crafts besides the 'free' and 'rough' masons already mentioned. There were also imagers, carvers, setters, wallers, paviours, tilers, quarriers, diggers; most of these completed apprenticeships of at least seven, often ten, years. From the ranks of these craftsmen evolved the 'master-masons' who could build and design as well as plan and manage. They also set up what were in effect schools of architecture in some of the bigger monasteries — for example at the Benedictine Abbey in Gloucester. In medieval times the credit for a building usually went to the instigator rather than the creator, to the abbot or the bishop rather than to the master-mason, so we do not know for certain the name of the genius

Right:
St Michael, Duntisbourne Rouse This is a tiny church on the hillside above its village on 'Dunt's' bourne or stream, a tributary of the Churn river that runs through Cirencester on its way to join the infant Thames at Cricklade. Who Dunt was, we don't know but the Rouse probably denotes that the manor was once the property of some otherwise unrecorded red-headed Norman lord. For this little church is a superb example of the enduring nature of Cotswld stone and with it, Cotswold village life. The nave has Saxon 'long and short' work: note the massive stones at the corners, and the herringbone masonry. The chancel and the crypt under it – not visible here – are Norman; the saddle-back tower is 'Perpendicular' with its upper part dated 1585; the mutilated churchyard cross on the right is 14th century, while the box tombs are 17th and 18th centuries and some have their inscriptions engraved on brass plates and set into matrices in the stone – a local Cotswold art that died out at the end of the last century.

who designed the choir of Gloucester Abbey. Some authorities believe it was one John de Sponlee of Winchcombe; others that it was 'Thomas of Gloucester' who became King's Master-mason to Edward III in London in 1353. This example from Gloucester demonstrates the innovative skill of the medieval masons working at just one of the many monasteries in the Cotswold region. Others would have been found at the other great monastic establishments. Thus there existed in the Cotswold region an innovative and highly skilled force of builders from late Norman times onwards. Only the money varied and the 13th century and early 14th century were not especially prosperous except, of course, for the monasteries who owned most of the sheep and which continued to expand and proliferate. (Lacock Abbey was built c1250.) Much of the early Gothic building in the Cotswolds was lost with the destruction of the abbeys of Winchcombe, Hailes and Cirencester but delightful examples can be found in both Gloucester Cathedral and Tewkesbury Abbey as well as at Lacock and Malmesbury. At the parish level, the 'Early English' period of the 13th century saw the building of chancels with lancet windows on to smaller and earlier naves and the introduction of stone bellcotes and primitive saddleback or gabled towers. The 'Decorated' style whose introduction covered the period of the Black Death is hardly represented in the Cotswolds at all, but during the early 14th century a number of notable church spires were built — Burford, Cheltenham, Stroud, Stanton, Saintbury and Sapperton among them.

The mid-14th century onwards saw the onset of the great period of Cotswold prosperity, based first on the wool trade and from about 1400 on the production of finished cloth. The Cotswolds became one vast sheep walk and flocks of 1,500 sheep and upwards were commonplace. Gloucester Abbey alone had a flock of 10,000 sheep in 1300. By the middle of the 14th century, England was exporting some 30,000 bales of wool a year which suggests that the sheep population was well over six million — and the Cotswolds were a major producer. The area too had many advantages when the trade changed from the export of raw wool to the production of cloth. Besides the sheep walks there was also an abundance of swift-running clear-water streams for washing and later on, water power — especially in the Frome and Avon valleys. Fuller's earth for degreasing could be found in the quarries. Teasels for raising the knap and woad for dyeing grew in the valleys and there was easy access to Bristol, the principal port for cloth exports. The fortunes made from the export of wool not only provided capital for the growing cloth industry but also created a new rich class of manufacturers and merchants — the woolmen. While the abbots used their wealth to undertake ambitious schemes of reconstruction to ancient foundations like Hailes, the great woolmen used theirs to improve the villages and rural parishes. They built houses great and small and in many places built or remodelled churches of spectacular magnificence in the Perpendicular style, among them Cirencester, Northleach, Chipping Campden, Winchcombe, Fairford, Calne, Cricklade and Lechlade. Of especial note are the church towers, often with diagonal buttresses, string courses and long narrow tracery panels, battlemented or traceried parapets with tall corner pinnacles.

But even in the smaller humbler village churches the masonry is often of the highest quality. Ashlar walling — regular sized blocks laid with narrow joints — is quite commonplace. Even where the masonry is coursed or random rubble — stones set into walls more or less as they are found — the corners and the window frames are ashlared. Commonplace too are handsome porches, ornamental parapets — even gargoyles — and that particular Cotswold feature, hood moulds over the windows, dropped down a few inches and then returned into a decorative stop. Most of the roofs are of tilestone and the windows are set in stone mullions. Window and door openings gradually became less pointed with the increasing use of the flatter four-centre and Tudor arches later in the period although window lights kept their pointed shape.

These then are the basic ingredients of what we know as the Cotswold style. And when the masons who built the churches went on to build the houses around them they followed similar practices. The Dissolution of the monasteries during the reign of Henry VIII under the Acts of 1536 and 1539 saw the total destruction of the monastic buildings at Hailes, Winchcombe and Cirencester and the sale of others

Left:
Great Chalfield Manor, Melksham Rebuilt in Corsham stone by Thomas Tropenell, a wealthy wool merchant, in c1480, Great Chalfield Manor is one of the most perfect of the surviving late medieval manor houses in the country. This is Cotswold stone – Corsham stone is of the 'Bath' variant of Great Oolite – displaying the Cotswold Tudor Gothic domestic style with is ecclesiastical antecedents only too apparent. The manor forms a neat complex of house, farm buildings and church all enclosed in a moat. The house is asymmetric and of the medieval 'great hall' type. It faces north – the sun and the south wind were considered unhealthy until well into the 17th century. The north front seen here has been virtually untouched since 1480 and has the hall windows in the middle with the hall chimney breast to the east (left) of them. The two gables from the hall have nave bay windows on one side and the porch on the other and both have diagonal buttresses – a Perpendicular feature as are the four-centred arches of the door and window openings. The two wings are again gabled and have charming oriel windows. A particular feature of the skyline are the delightful gable finials, intricately carved figures of griffins and knights in armour. That they have survived unscathed for 500 years in an exposed position shows the durability of the Corsham variety of oolite. Greville's House in Chipping Campden is the urban equivalent of Chalfield.

like Lacock as well as monastic lands and outlying granges — Broadway is an example — to those who could afford them. Although in execution the 'Dissolution' was callous, arbitrary and often brutal it was in effect a great act of 'privatisation' and the consequences were similar — more money in private hands and a sharp expansion of the economy. The religious Reformation that followed brought an effective end to church building and there are few post-Reformation churches in the Cotswolds earlier than about 1700. But the stone was still there and so was the money. The masons released from monastic and ecclesiastical tasks were available to build private houses. And build they did, not only great 'prodigy' houses for the courtiers and landed gentry and farmhouses for the growing class of yeomen farmers, but many smaller houses in the expanding towns and villages. The period between about 1570 and 1640 is often referred to by architectural historians as the 'Great Rebuilding' when building activity throughout the country rose to a peak. It involved, however, not only the creation of more houses but of much better ones in terms of quality of accommodation. In this respect the 'Great Rebuilding' marks the change from medieval communal living to modern living with its emphasis on individual privacy. Simple hall houses became L-shaped or added further wings to become H- or E-shaped. Ceilings were inserted in open halls and bedrooms went upstairs, parlours were no longer used as sleeping quarters, open hearth fires were replaced by fireplaces and chimneys and service rooms like kitchens, bakehouses and brewhouses, hitherto external, were moved into the main house. Farmhouses which in earlier times would have accommodated all the farm's workers in their open halls became the preserve of the farmer's family and separate cottages and bothies were built for labourers — primitive at first but later often improving. This steady transition occurred all over the country whatever the building material used. However, fashion required an increased use of stone for bigger houses and many timber-framed buildings were sheathed in stone or given stone fronts at this time. In the Cotswolds it was quite usual for special quarries to be dug to build single houses and the fact is often recorded in local field names used to this day: Stone Pit Close and Stone Acre Meadow are examples. The period saw the establishment of the traditional Cotswold stone farmhouse in what is essentially an Elizabethan 'Gothic' style which has, with local variations, been the prototype of houses great and small all along the stone belt ever since.

The use of stone tiles for roofing calls for strong rafters and a steep pitch to the roof if the rain isn't to find its way through the gaps between the rather unevenly-faced tilestones. The usual pitch is 45°-50° but in older buildings, 60° even 65° is not uncommon. This means, of course, that there is a good deal of roof space and whilst this is acceptable in a church, a barn, or even a medieval hall house with its open hearth, it could not be wasted in the new demand for multiple rooms. Besides the fitting of dormer windows, a particular Cotswold solution was to raise the house front in a series of separate subsidiary gables set side by side, often almost touching each other, along the parapet and each with its own ridge the same height as the main roof. Since steep-pitched roofs require gable ends as well — hipped roofs are comparatively rare at this period — the prominent gable is the key characteristic of Cotswold architecture either on individual houses or multiplied an hundredfold in villages and towns. The other main characteristic is the Cotswold window — stone mullions carefully shaped and joined supporting a stone lintel across several lights, four perhaps on the ground floor, three on the first floor and two in the gable. The casements are of wrought iron and until the end of the 17th century, the glass was lead-mounted in diamond-shaped panes. Later, until the end of the 18th century, rectangular panes were more usual. The window is surmounted by a horizontal hood mould called a 'label' which drops at the ends and often turns into a decorated label stop — just as they did earlier around the Gothic windows of churches. Quite often too, where there is series of windows, the labels are run together in what is called a 'string-course', in effect a drip stone running right round the house. 'Gables, labels, lintels and lights' could perhaps thus sum up our basic Cotswold domestic style.

There are also, of course, other refinements which often reflect contemporary taste. Gables usually have verges — the tiles of the gables end in a parapet from the gable wall rather than jut out, bonnet fashion. The gable itself is often crowned by an ornamental finial — a ball, a flambeau or some local creation depending again upon the period and the artistic whim of the local mason. In the north Cotswolds gable walls are also often used for decorative purposes with date stones,

Right:
Old Manor, Aston-sub-Edge Gables, labels, lintels, lights and chimneys set diagonally – this old manor house was built in the enduring Cotswold style early in the 17th century like Shipton Court (p27) but on a smaller scale. Note the ball finials on the gables. Notice too the short length of timber-framed wall on the right which suggests that this house too may have replaced an earlier one of different construction. A long gallery runs from end to end like those found in houses of the same period. (Chastleton (p39) and Broughton (p41) are examples.) The house first belonged to the Porter family, Edmund Porter of Aston who married his cousin Angela Porter of Mickleton. Their son, born in 1587, was Endymion Porter, a patron of the poets Herrick and Ben Jonson and one of Charles I's ambassadors. He entertained Prince Rupert here for the famous Dover's Games at Chipping Campden.

escutcheons, oval windows and the like. Chimneys are usually found at the end of buildings often with the stacks set diagonally to the axis of the roof. Except in the larger houses and in towns, large bay windows are comparatively rare except as later additions, often Victorian. One attractive and particular Cotswold feature, however, is the ground floor bay with a stone base and a stone tiled roof. Doorways tend to have four-centre or Tudor arches and from the late Elizabethan period onwards, porches with Classical motifs — columns and pediments — are often featured and houses become more symmetrical. The Old Manor at Aston-sub-Edge, Chastleton and Shipton Court are examples.

This distinctive Cotswold vernacular style of architecture continued in use for many houses in the smaller towns and villages until well into the Georgian era and was revived again at the end of the 19th century by numerous architects associated with the arts and crafts movement begun by William Morris with its emphasis on traditional styles, materials and craftsmanship. And even today, vestiges of the traditional 'Cotswold Style' are to be found in the design of modern 'executive' housing — gables, labels, lintels and lights — even if the Cotswold stone often used is first crushed, mixed with cement and precast into the required shapes. Nowadays we have the stone and we have the money but stonemasons are in short supply.

If the traditional 'Cotswold' style of building came up from the bottom, from the 'Gothic' craft of local masons, the Classical style which was in vogue nationally from the late 17th century until the mid-19th century came in from the top. The tone was set by the architects and builders of royal palaces like Whitehall and the Queen's House at Greenwich early in the 17th century — Inigo Jones is the prime example. The style was followed by courtiers for their great houses and by builders in fashionable towns and was then copied down the social scale by the trendsetters of the day. One of the earliest Renaissance houses was Chipping Campden Manor built in c1613 but largely destroyed in the Civil War. A more complete example is Charlton Park House. The Restoration saw an upsurge in building, much of it in the style of Classical architecture favoured in Holland which we know variously as 'William & Mary', 'Queen Anne' or 'Wren': compact, square houses often without wings; two main storeys set above a semi-basement; a bold eaves cornice below a hipped roof with attic windows; windows continued to be mullion and transom crossed with leaded panes until the end of the 17th century but sash windows came in from c1685 onwards. Quite often there would be a pediment over the entrance front but in general there was little decoration in early Stuart houses.

The arrival of the more flamboyant 'Baroque' style first into the colleges of Oxford and even more splendidly into Vanbrugh's Blenheim Palace at Woodstock was again echoed down the social ladder to smaller houses both in the country and in the prosperous clothier towns like Bradford-on-Avon and Painswick. One example was known as 'Bristol Baroque' and made use of columns or pilasters with pediments to emphasise doors and windows on the first and second floors. Westbury House is an example. By the 1740s, the more restrained 'Palladian' style so characteristic of the Georgian era had replaced the Baroque and it was in this style that the immensely fashionable 'new' spa town of Bath was built between 1750 and 1775. In essence in England the term 'Palladian' implies a house with a rectangular central block with three main storeys, low basement, deep second, narrower third; the central bay with a pediment and supporting columns or pilasters; a hipped roof with dormer windows behind the parapet; rectangular sash windows with multiple panes. An example is Lydiard Mansion. Again the Palladian influence spread across the surrounding area for large country houses and down the social scale in villages and small towns.

Late in the 18th century, royal patronage created a new spa in Cheltenham which was subsequently built in the more elaborate Greek-revivalist style we know as 'Regency' but still essentially Classical. This was of course the period of two passions among landowners and the urban rich: the love of the 'Picturesque' and the desire to bring the countryside into the town known as '*rus in urbe*'. The former passion meant making the house and its setting look like a painting by one of the landscape artists of the 17th century — Claude or Poussin — with ruined temples and grottoes in the background. *Rus in urbe* meant that although a house might be located in the middle of a town like Cheltenham, its appearance from both within and without was as if it were a country gentleman's house in the depths of the countryside.

All this was done against a background of unparalleled national prosperity of which the Cotswold region enjoyed its share. It was the time of the agricultural revolution of which a key feature was the process of enclosure, which meant that the communal field patterns and 'commons' of medieval origin were rather arbitrarily transferred into individual private hands sometimes by purchase, later by specific Acts of Parliament. The enclosed fields then provided a basic framework for the introduction of new and more productive — and profitable — methods of farming. In the Cotswolds the process of enclosure was at its height betweeen 1760 and 1830 and was virtually complete by about 1840. It was during this period that the hundreds of

Left:
Westbury House, Bradford-on-Avon The cloth trade in the Avon valley maintained the prosperity of towns like Bradford well into the 18th century and rich local clothiers were able to indulge their taste for fashionable houses in the increasingly popular Classical style. Westbury House is an example of a local style known as 'Bristol Baroque' which although the house was built c1730 owes more to the earlier rather ornate Queen Anne style of Blenheim than to the more austere Georgian style then coming into vogue. The house is built of local stone and the level of craftsmanship is very high. The main points of interest on the south front are the Ionic pilasters supporting a broken pediment on the ground floor, Corinthian pilasters on the second supporting another broken pediment, the pronounced keystones over the ground floor windows and the balustrading.

Left:
The Almshouses, Chipping Campden In his book in the well-known Pevsner series, David Verey describes this terrace as 'the crowning achievement of the Cotswold domestic style and mason craft of the early 17th century . . .' and who could doubt his judgement. The terrace was built in 1612 by a local benefactor, a City merchant, Sir Baptist Hicks (d1629) who bought the manor in 1609 and whose arms appear in the centre. It comprises 12 two-storey dwellings each suitably gabled with stone-mullioned windows, drip moulds on the upper storey and a string-course on the lower. The construction in local stone is of tightly jointed freestone blocks known as ashlar – and of the highest quality. (The almshouses were carefully restored in 1953.) Ironically perhaps, the manor house built by Sir Baptist – he later became Lord Campden – for his family at the same time did not survive him long. It was largely destroyed during the Civil War.

miles of drystone walling that are such a feature — despite some more recent removals — of the Cotswolds were built.

The second half of the 19th century saw a sharp decline in prosperity throughout the Cotswold region. Imports of cheap flour reduced the amount of arable land and more and more was put down to grass but no longer for sheep. The local wool trade had been in decline since the 18th century and cheap imports first from Germany and later from Australia virtually ended sheep farming in the Cotswolds and helped finally to bring to an end the historic Cotswold breed with its large joints and heavy fleeces. In the clothing industry competition from Yorkshire, a reluctance to change to steam power and an increasingly bloody-minded workforce put many firms out of business and the population of the towns and villages of the south and southwest Cotswolds steadily declined. Even in Cheltenham, Victorian prudery steadily drove out Regency revelry and the fine houses became vacant and the hordes of servants unemployed. Cheltenham was saved first by its growing educational facilities and then by the attraction of its fine — and cheap — houses and plentiful domestics to well-heeled 'nabobs' of all types returning on retirement from the Raj — what is usually known as its 'curry and colonels' era. Later it became what it is now, a major centre for commerce and light industry of all kinds and its legacy of superb Regency buildings has never looked better than it does today.

The Cotswolds themselves benefited from the growth of tourism which came in with the motor vehicle and the steady if somewhat erratic improvement in the fortunes of the agricultural industry since the two world wars. Until very recently arable crops predominated and the landscape was full of growing corn interspersed with golden fields of oilseed rape. Now there seems again to be more grass on the hilltops and the sheep are back again in their thousands.

In the pages that follow, what we have done is to 'follow the oolite', as Massingham would have said, around its main body in the Cotswolds and not only in the physical-geography sense but also in the stylistic sense. The region covered by this book thus goes well beyond what some purists would accept as the *real* Cotswolds — the Cherwell valley, Oxford, even Bath and the valley of the Avon. We have done this to show how pervasive the Cotswold style has been all along the stone belt and had we taken Massingham's precedent, we could have extended the 'Cotswold Country' from Devon to Lincolnshire but that perhaps is for another book another day. What we have covered is the 'Greater Cotswolds' — from Banbury to Bath, from Oxford to Cheltenham, Chipping Campden to Chippenham. This then is a portrait of the Cotswold region as seen by one of Europe's greatest photographers of our heritage. What I as editor and author have endeavoured to do is to point out what is of interest and significance in the photographs and, since the Cotswolds have an unrivalled folklore of myths and legends, to look occasionally into some of the stories behind them. For those who would know more of Cotswold stone, Cotswold style or Cotswold history, there is a detailed bibliography at the end.

Alan Hollingsworth
The Hollyhocks

1
Oxfordshire

Right:
Oxford skyline seen from Boar's Hill It was the Victorian poet, Matthew Arnold, scholar of Balliol (1841), Fellow of Oriel (1845) and Professor of Poetry (1857) who created the most used and abused image of Oxford's 'dreaming spires'. He also wrote:

And bower me from the August sun with shade;
And the eye travels down to Oxford's Towers.
From *The Scholar-Gipsy*, 1836

He may well have been thinking of the panorama seen here, a favourite for centuries. Oxford Dons and sundry poets have lived in the pleasant suburb of Boar's Hill, John Masefield and Robert Bridges among them. The hill itself is 536ft (176m) high — 50ft was added earlier this century when an artificial mound was built by the celebrated archaeologist and Keeper of the Ashmolean Museum in Oxford, Sir Arthur Evans (d1941), to give an uninterrupted view round his home. He made it a sanctuary for wild flowers. Although no one would say that Oxford is a Cotswold city, the majority of its older buildings are of Cotswold stone and like those of Lower Slaughter, they light up in the August sunlight. Clearly visible here is Wren's Tom Tower with the Radcliffe Camera behind it. Magdalen Tower stands out on the right.

Right:
Tom Tower, Christ Church College, Oxford
Perhaps the most distinctive of 'Oxford's Towers', Tom Tower with its ogee cap is mostly the work of Sir Christopher Wren in 1681-82. Christ Church — usually known as 'The House' — was founded by Cardinal Wolsey in 1525 and he used the King's master-masons, Lubbyn and Redman, to build it. The lower part of Tom Tower in the Tudor Perpendicular Gothic style of Wolsey's day was left uncompleted — a style adopted and inevitably adapted by Wren for the rest of the tower out of deference to the founder. Gothic it is but not so busy as the original lower down and more Wren perhaps than Tudor. The five light windows over the gateway with their ogee gables — there is one either side — have niches with, on this side, a statue of Cardinal Wolsey and, on the other, of Queen Anne. Tom Tower takes its name from 'Great Tom', a six-ton bell that once hung in nearby Osney Abbey and was recast in 1680. Its function?

Tingle, Tingle, Tingle,
Says the little bell at 9
To call the beerers home
But devill the man
Will leave his Can
Till he hears the mighty Tome.
Henry Aldrich, c1670

'Mighty Tome' still rings at five past nine each evening the 101 chimes that once served as a curfew for members of the college.

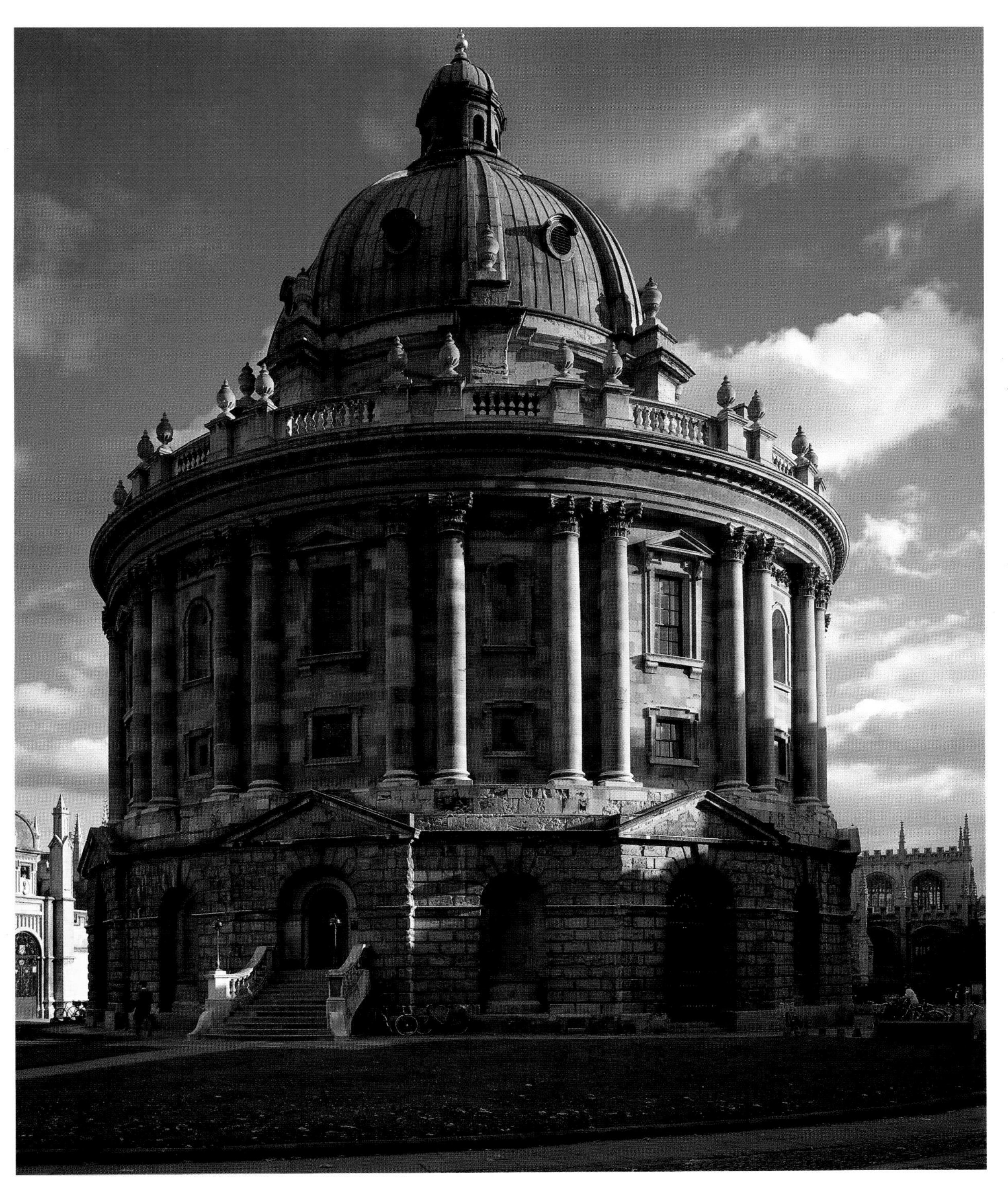

Left:
Radcliffe Camera, Oxford A University statute in 1863 decreed that 'the building known till lately as the Radcliffe Library is now used as a Reading Room in connection with the Bodleian Library under the name of *Camera Bodleiana*' — the word 'camera' in this case being used in its Latin sense of an arched or vaulted chamber but implying nothing optical at all. It is still used as a reading room for the Bodleian Library to which it is linked by a tunnel and a conveyor belt, but Radcliffe's name has prevailed. Dr John Radcliffe (1650-1714) was a prominent London physician renowned for his candid approach to his patients. He is said to have told Queen Anne that there was nothing wrong with her but the 'vapours' and he declined to attend her on her deathbed. Nonetheless he left a great deal of money — £40,000 for what was originally intended to be a medical library, £30,000 for the Radcliffe Observatory and £6,000 towards the Radcliffe Infirmary. Between Radcliffe's death and the money becoming available in 1736, a number of the architects of the day put forward ideas for a library building in the shape of a rotunda, Wren and Hawksmoor among them. The task was finally given to James Gibbs (1682-1754), the designer of St Martin-in-the Fields, and the library was built between 1737 and 1748. His building has a strong rusticated base, pairs of tall Corinthian columns supporting a balustraded parapet topped by urns. This is capped by a dome and lantern which are among the finest in Britain and another distinctive addition to Oxford's skyline. In style it is a blending of Wren's Baroque and the rather mannered Palladianism Gibbs learned in Rome where he studied in 1703-09. It was highly attractive to 18th century architects and Gibbs' *Book of Architecture* (1728) is said to have influenced the builders of the White House in Washington. Gibbs' greatest glory is inside the buiding — the magnificent spiral staircase with its superb ironwork in Swedish iron. It cost all of £168 10s — which gives us a perspective of the value in those days of Dr Radcliffe's endowments.

Right:
Schools Quadrangle, Bodleian Library, Oxford
Sir Nikolaus Pevsner considers it to be one of the finest buildings in England and instructs the visitor 'on arrival turn back at once; for such a frontispiece as this one will never see again. With five tiers it is the biggest in England and that means anywhere.' The Bodleian Library is named after Sir Thomas Bodley (1545-1613), an English diplomat and book-collector who served in embassies in Europe between 1580 and 1597 and amassed many books. In 1598 he returned to Oxford where he had been a Fellow, refounded the medieval university library and spent the remainder of his life restoring it. The library began in 1602 with 2,000 books, but Bodley made an arrangement with the Stationers' Hall that a copy of every book published and registered should be placed in it. The arrangement has continued to the present day when the Bodleian is still a copyright library. It now has more than 3,500,000 volumes as well as thousands of manuscripts. The Schools Quadrangle was built in 1613-24 at a time when the Classical style was only just being introduced in England. The gate tower is a late medieval building, essentially Gothic in style but the stages each carry columns of the Classical Order from Tuscan at ground level, through Roman Doric, Ionic and Corinthian to Composite. This unusual embellishment may have been the result of Bodley's own influence.

Above:
Magdalen College Tower, Oxford Founded in 1458 by William of Waynflete, Bishop of Winchester, on the site of the 13th century St John's Hospital, Magdalen is one of the largest and most beautiful of the Oxford colleges. With its deer-park setting and its riverside walks it has been said that it combines the dignity of a college with the magnificence of a country seat. Especially attractive are its medieval limestone buildings grouped around the cloister — a reminder that most of the earlier colleges were, in effect, monastic establishments at least in design and structure and most subjects taught were theological. Student activities then as now, however, were anything but monastic. An inspection carried out by the then Bishop of Winchester in 1507 reported the following misdemeanours:

Stokes was unchaste with the wife of a tailor.
Stokysley baptised a cat and practised witchcraft.
Gregory climbed the great gate by the Tower, and brought a Stranger into College.
Kendall wears a gown not sewn together in front.

Does anything important really change in Oxford?

Magdalen Tower, completed in 1509, is in the Perpendicular style and its upper stage resembles that of many a Cotswold 'wool-church'. It is here that the choristers sing their traditional Latin hymn *Te Deum Patrem Colinus* at sunrise each May Day morning — and not in celebration of Karl Marx: he was not an Oxford man.

Right:
Minster Lovell Hall, Oxon The impressive remains of a medieval house built c1431-32 in a charming setting on the banks of the Windrush and carefully tended by English Heritage. The house was set around three sides of a courtyard with the fourth side fronting the river enclosed by a buttressed wall. Despite a demolition carried out c1747, enough of the buildings have survived to give a clear idea of the extent of the house. Seen here is the shell of the former great hall, high in comparison to its length and width with tall windows in which some traces of medieval tracery remain. This open hall would have provided accommodation for the numerous retainers — the lord and lady had their own private solars — who ate and slept around an open hearth fire, the smoke rising into the rafters to drift out through the holes still visible in the gable. Minster Lovell Hall is famous for two legends — probably one engendered the other. The one is that in 1718 when the house was being repaired, a vaulted room was discovered which contained the seated skeleton of a man with the skeleton of a dog at his feet. It was generally assumed to have been that of Francis Lovell — ironically known as 'Lovell the Dog' — a Yorkist who fought on the losing side at the battles of Bosworth in 1485 and Stoke in 1487. He is believed to have escaped to Lovell Hall and hidden himself away in a locked room later to starve to death when his only servant died. The second legend, that of the 'Mistletoe Bough', is of a bride playing hide-and-seek on her wedding night who hides in a box with a heavy lid, finds herself trapped, starves to death and is not found until years later . . . This story, however, has other claimants beside Minster Lovell, but at Minster Lovell at dusk it is easy to accept either or both of these old tales.

Right:
Shipton Court, Shipton-under-Wychwood, Oxon One of the largest Jacobean houses in the country, Shipton Court was built for the Lacey family in 1603. Although its tall gable-topped bays with their kneelers and finials and its blocks of chimneys are still very much in the tradition of Tudor domestic Gothic, this west front is strictly symmetrical. Other parts of the house are not: the east front has only four gables and a battlemented stair turret. This suggests that it was a remodelling of an earlier house on the same site — possibly timber-framed. Oak was plentiful in the old Wychwood forest in medieval times and the period of the 'great rebuilding' saw many timber-framed houses rebuilt in fashionable stone. The mullioned windows with their bracket moulds are modern but in keeping — more so than the sash windows they apparently replaced. Wychwood itself was one of the five 'Domesday Forests' and became a royal hunting preserve. During the Napoleonic wars much of the timber was felled and later in the 19th century it was enclosed and cultivated.

Right:
St John the Baptist, Burford With its neighbour Northleach, Burford was described about 1400 as one of the most important wool-markets in the Cotswolds, a role it continued to fulfil until the early 16th century. This long period of prosperity is reflected in the complexities of the architecture of its church. Of the original Norman church all that remains is the central tower — indicated by the round-arched former bell opening with the zigzag mouldings — and the west wall of the nave. The main remodelling came in the 15th century with the funds provided by the wool merchants. The wide Perpendicular windows, the panelled and pinnacled porch and the spire and the upper stage of the tower are all of this period, as are many of the chantry chapels. That on the left of the porch is of particular interest. It was originally a separate Lady Chapel founded by the Guild of Merchants in 1200. After the Reformation it ceased to be used liturgically and was taken over by one of the local wool merchants for family tombs and became known as the 'Sylvester' aisle. (It is now a Lady Chapel again.) One of the family, Thomas Sylvester, supported the King during the Civil War and doubtless lost his family fortune as a result, but the Sylvester aisle was to play its part in national history in 1649. In May of that year a regiment of the Parliamentary army based in Salisbury espoused the Levellers' cause, mutinied and marched northwards. It took up quarters in the Burford area where it was surprised by loyal forces under Cromwell and Fairfax. After a brief struggle the mutineers surrendered and about 400 were imprisoned in Burford church. Next morning, 19 May 1649, a cornet and two corporals were court-martialled, stood against the church wall and shot. Their comrades were lined up on the leads of the Sylvester aisle to learn a salutary lesson. Cromwell pardoned them the decimation they deserved and the Levellers rebellion was at an end.

Above:
The Great Barn, Coxwell This enormous building dwarfs the large farmhouse beside it and was a landmark on its hillside above the airfield at Watchfield that even a beginner pilot could not mistake from the air. As Massingham observes, this great Gothic cathedral of a barn is really Berkshire's — removed by the infamous 1974 Act — and was that county's only notable building built of Cotswold stone. It was built by the monks of Beaulieu Abbey in c1204 when King John was on the throne and thus may well pre-date Magna Carta. It is 152ft (50m) long, 44ft (15m) wide and 48ft (16m) high. Its stone tiles came from the Stonesfield quarry and it still has the original massive oak timbering to support them. The only major alterations are the large doors at the ends which were put in during the 18th century to admit bigger wagons. The mushroom-shaped stones in the foreground are another use for the easily-shaped Cotswold stone. Known as 'staddles' or in some places 'dottles', they were used with planks of wood to lift the bases of hayricks and cornstacks off the ground. Now they are used merely as ornaments. The barn has been owned by the National Trust since 1956 and is open to the public throughout the year.

NO ENTRY
PLEASE DO NOT
CLIMB ON THE
GATES

Previous page:
Blenheim Palace, Woodstock As John Vanbrugh, the architect of Blenheim, explained to the Duchess of Marlborough when Blenheim Palace was being built in 1709, 'there happened one great disappointment. The Freestone in the Park Quarry not proving good which if it had would have saved 50 per cent in that article.' (He was, of course, talking about money — a continuous cause of friction with the Duchess.) Blenheim is 'off the oolite' and stands on an outcrop of inferior stone. As a result throughout the building of the Palace, stone had to be brought in by horse and cart from over 20 quarries in the Cotswold area, those at Taynton and Barrington among them. One story says that there are still massive blocks of Great Oolite in the woods in Wychwood Forest awaiting collection. At the Duchess's insistence Vanbrugh had to use some local stone from Glympton in the Kitchen Court; it is now in decay. (When the Duchess finally moved into the Palace — still not complete — in 1719, she complained bitterly that the stone was bad for her gout.) Vanbrugh was the supreme exponent of the Baroque Classical style in its English form and Blenheim and the Oxford colleges in similar style set a fashion that was copied down the social scale over the next 20 years. (See also pp32-35.)

Right:
The Great Court, Blenheim Palace The site and surrounding estate together with a grant towards the cost of building a great palace were given to the first Duke of Marlborough by Queen Anne (reigned 1702-14) and a grateful government as a national monument to his victory over the French at Blenheim in Bavaria in 1704. The architect chosen — some say by the Queen, others by the Duke himself — was John Vanbrugh (1664-1726), a successful playwright who had taken up architecture 'without thought or lecture' as Jonathan Swift put it. In fact Vanbrugh had by that date already demonstrated his genius as an architect in the design of Castle Howard in Yorkshire (which latter-day TV watchers will know better as 'Brideshead'). He also had as his assistant another architect of genius — and a fully trained one — in Nicholas Hawksmoor (1661-1736). They were both exponents of a style of Classical architecture known as 'Baroque'. What this means is that the style is not that of the strict Classical architecture known to the ancients but a romantic idea of what it might have been — in other words, a free expression of the Classical idea with imagination and ingenuity given full reign. When the imagination in question was that of a Restoration playwright the result was certain to be spectacular. (This Great Court, for example, has been likened to an enormous stage set.) The result is that Blenheim is regarded as the supreme expression of the English Baroque. Three aspects of Vanbrugh's personal style are apparent here — the broken skyline, 'ups and downs'; the projections and recessions, 'ins and outs'; and the use of 'eminencies' — roof-top towers, pinnacles and statues to draw attention to the roofline, an echo of Elizabethan Perpendicular Gothic.

Right:
West Front and Water Terrace Garden, Blenheim Palace One of Vanbrugh's romantic ideas was to impart to his buildings what he called a 'castle air'. His arcaded rooftop corner towers looking like City church lanterns — Hawksmoor probably designed them — helped to contribute to this 'air' surmounted as they are by pinnacles composed of cannonballs, reversed fleur-de-lys — the French emblem insultingly standing on its head — with a ducal coronet at the very top. Although Vanbrugh and Hawksmoor had suggested a water garden here it was not made until the ninth Duke of Marlborough (d1934) determined to give Blenheim Palace the magnificent formal setting originally intended for it. With the help of Achille Duchene, he created the splendid garden seen here against many difficulties during the years 1925-30. He also laid out new gardens on the north and east fronts.

2 Warwickshire & Worcestershire

Right:
Rousham House, Steeple Aston Rousham has remained in family hands since it was built, in this case, the family is the Cotterel-Dormers. Indeed the Dormers go back further than the house; Jane Dormer was lady-in-waiting to Mary Tudor. Built in c1635 by Sir Robert Dormer – a Royalist – the house was fortified by putting musket loop-holes in the front door. When built the house probably had gables and finials, mullions and labels in the Tudor Gothic style of the time. A century later, General Sir James Dormer, a friend of Alexander Pope and Jonathan Swift, had the house and garden remodelled by William Kent (1685-1748), an early exponent of the Romantic 'Picturesque' movement which revolutionised the relationship between house and landscape. Rousham House was restyled as an Early Tudor Gothic palace with battlements and windows glazed with octagonal panes. He also added the low side wings and threw in a few Classical details – dentil cornices and a pediment or two – for good measure. The garden was well ahead of its time – the Picturesque did not reach its full flowering until the end of the 18th century – and the only surviving example of Kent's landscape design. Making full use of the River Cherwell that runs through the grounds, he laid out a Classical garden with all the ingredients that Claude or Poussin might have put into their pictures: glades and grottoes, statues, cascades and cupids, Venus, ponds and pyramids, watery walks and eye-catchers. Rousham House and garden is open to the public during the summer months.

Right:
Chastleton House We are back with gables, labels, lintels and lights at the time (c1608) when the Perpendicular Gothic of the Tudor period was becoming influenced by Classical ideas. The house is symmetrical about the central bay with projecting bays on either side stepping back to flanking staircase towers. The gables have tall finials and pinnacles on the kneelers to emphasise the vertical aspect and give a dramatic roofline. There are, however, Classical motifs around the doorway, a triangular pediment over the top window of the central bay and another over the gateway. The house was built by a Witney wool merchant, Walter Jones, who purchased the estate from Robert Catesby, one of the instigators of the infamous Gunpowder Plot, and some sources say that money from the sale went to further the Plot. The Jones family however were devoted Royalists – one of them hid in a secret room in the house after escaping from the battle of Worcester in 1651 – and although the direct line died out in 1828, the house is still in descendants' hands and has never been sold. The result is that it has been little altered internally over the centuries – the Long Gallery at the back of the house is of special interest. The house also contains much of its original panelling, furniture and artefacts. It is open to the public during the summer months.

Right:
Broughton Castle This house was built of Middle Lias or marlstone from the famous quarry at Hornton about seven miles away with its deep brown, tawny yellow and greenish tints. But we are now 'off the oolite' and hence out of the true Cotswold stone region but not out of the style. John de Broughton built a stone manor house and chapel on a moated site here in c1300 but the licence to crenellate which made it a castle in name if not in structure was not granted until 1405 and to Sir Thomas Wykeham. He added the battlements and the arrow slits and fortified the gatehouse. In 1451 a Wykeham grand-daughter married William Fiennes, second Baron Saye and Sele, who died fighting at the battle of Barnet in 1471 and the house has remained the property of the Fiennes family ever since. The eighth baron and first Viscount Saye and Sele was a party to the conspiracy which engineered the Civil War and there is a room high up in the house where the instigators met – Pym, Hampden, Vane, Brooke, Warwick, Best and Essex among them. Celia Fiennes (1662-1741) the traveller and diarist was also a member of the family. The old medieval courtyard house was modernised in the Tudor period, c1551, when the battlements were removed and gables put in, a floor was inserted into the great hall, chimneys replaced open hearths and staircase towers were added together with massive mullioned bay windows on the north, entrance, front. At the same time the interior was brought up to the Elizabethan standards of privacy and comfort. Seen here is the south front – most medieval houses faced north – with the battlemented medieval solar east wing on the right with its 14th century two-light window, the two gabled staircase towers at either end of the great hall. Between them with an original buttress embedded in it is the hall chimney breast. Little was done to the house in the succeeding centuries. The Fiennes adherence to the Parliamentary cause saved the castle during the Civil War and it mercifully escaped the attention of the Victorian restorers. It is open to the public in the summer months.

Right:
St Mary's Church, Bloxham One of the grandest churches in Oxfordshire, St Mary's enjoyed royal patronage until the Dissolution when it passed to Eton College. The original Norman church was enlarged in the 12th century with an Early English nave and aisles. These aisles were enlarged and a chancel rebuilt during the Decorated period. The tower and spire with their splendid carving were built c1340 and the large Perpendicular style east windows – seen here on the left – were put in during the building of the Milcombe Chapel in the 15th century. There was a major restoration of the church, inevitably, in 1864-66 and the east window of the chancel dates from that time. However, as the glass in these great windows is by William Morris, the founder of the Society for the Protection of Ancient Buildings – set up to fight the Victorian 'improvers' – and Burne-Jones, c1869, the actual 'scraping' by G. E. Street must have been acceptable to them. The similarity of the fine churches of this area – Bloxham, Adderbury and King's Sutton – suggests that the same masons may have worked on all three. Legend has it that they were built by three brothers and an anonymous and highly industrious assistant who turned out to be the devil. In fact, the architect of the 15th century work on several of the churches in this area is thought to have been a master-mason called Richard Winchcombe who designed and built the Divinity School in Oxford in 1430.

Previous page:
Abbot Lichfield's Bell Tower, Evesham The Benedictine Abbey of Evesham was founded in 701AD and occupied a large site on the banks of the Avon where, it is said, Eoves the Swineherd first saw a vision of the Virgin Mary. Over the centuries it grew in wealth and importance and the market town of Evesham prospered outside its walls. Abbot Lichfield was the last of its abbots and it was he who built this free-standing belfry. With its boldly projecting and stepped buttresses, its finely wrought decoration culminating in the lavish carving of the parapet and pinnacles, it is a perfect example of Cotswold Perpendicular. It is also the last. It was begun – in 1529 – at a time when the monasteries were already under critical scrutiny, not all of it royal, for the opulence and extravagance of their life style. Its sheer lavishness made it an ill-timed exercise in what we would nowadays call 'conspicuous expenditure' – the abbot is said to have paid for it himself. He also built himself a chantry chapel and endowed the local grammar school. He resigned when the abbey was dissolved in 1540 rather than hand it over to the King's Commissioners and died in 1546. At the Dissolution the great abbey church and most of the monastic building were taken down leaving only the two gatehouses, some lesser buildings and this tower. There are two parish churches on the site, the one on the right is All Saints. The one one the left is St Lawrence's which has another chapel built by Abbot Lichfield on its south side. The abbey grounds are accessible to the public at all times.

Right:
The Almonry Museum, Evesham This is a medieval house partly in stone and partly timber-framed as is fitting to a location on the very edge of the Cotswolds where the two building traditions meet. Apart from the mullioned window, however, the stone is not the usual oolite but appears to be Blue Lias which is not a freestone and cannot be ashlared. The timber-framed half is 'close-studded' – its vertical timbers close together, a building style usually found only on high quality buildings in this part of England. The square-panelling seen on the right is more usual. The blacking of the timbers and the whitening of the infilling is a Victorian affectation. Besides its abbey, Evesham is famous for the battle fought on a hill north of the town in 1265. There Edward, Prince of Wales – later Edward I – defeated the rebel barons under Simon de Montfort and his son both of whom were slain in the battle, together, it is said, with 18 barons, 160 knights and 4,000 men-at-arms. Simon de Montfort's remains were buried secretly in the abbey. The Almonry Museum covers all Evesham's long history and is open during the summer months.

Right:
St Eadburgh's Church, Broadway Until the coaches came in the 17th century, the main road from Worcester to London went up the escarpment past this church and through Middle Hill instead of through the village high street as it does today. The village at that time was much less 'linear' than it is now and was grouped around the green and to the south of it where this church lies. Until the Dissolution it was, from 972AD, one of the granges of the Benedictine Abbey of Pershore – a country seat for the abbot whose house is still standing on the Green, produce and profit for the abbey and a hospice for sickly monks. It became Crown property in 1539 and was sold in 1558 to the Babington family. The Elizabethan manor house Broadway Court was demolished in 1773 and only its Gatehouse is still standing, a few yards from this church. The church itself is Norman in origin, largely 12th century and 14th century in construction but with the usual Perpendicular additions of windows and battlements.

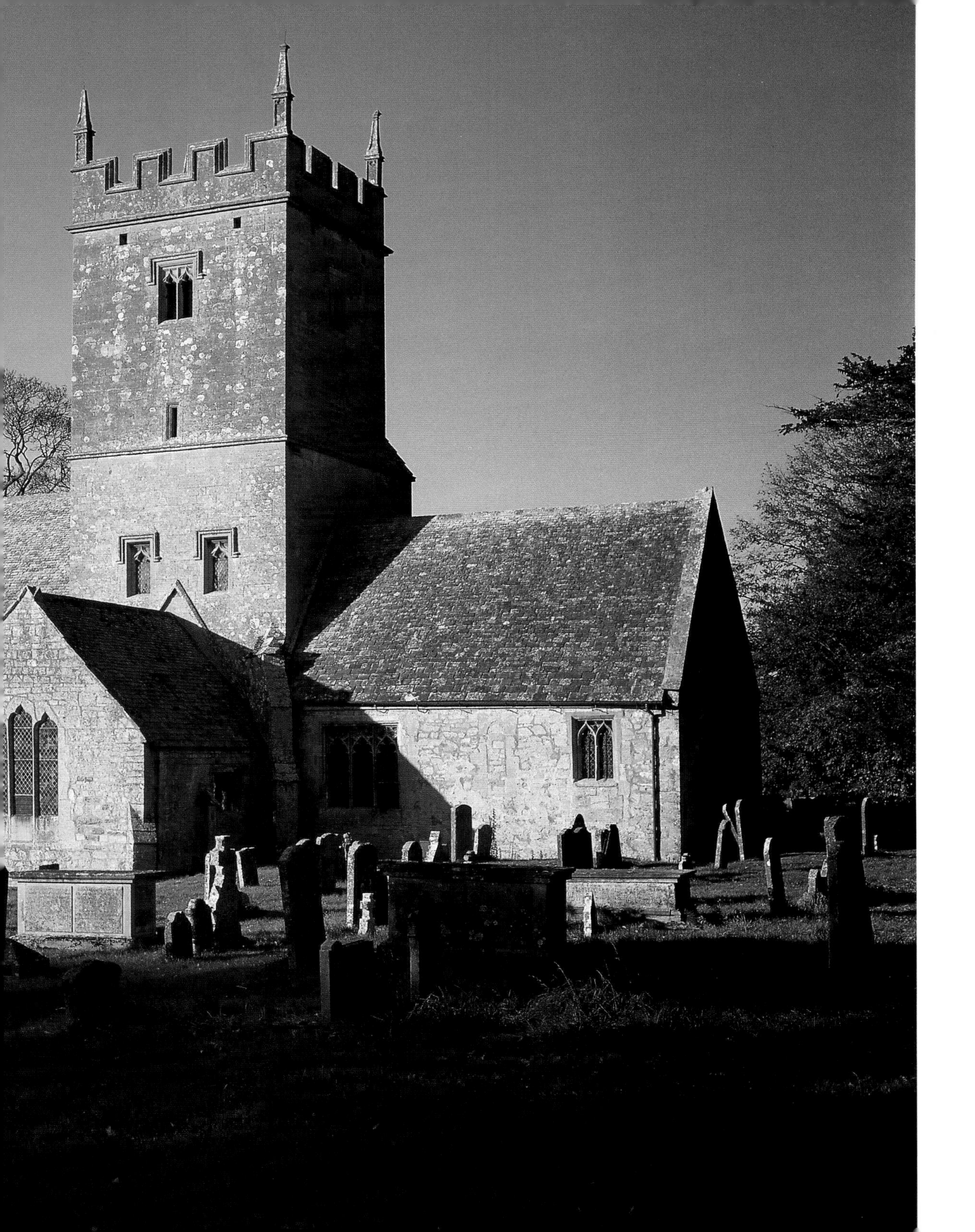

3
Gloucestershire

Right:
Neptune's Fountain, The Promenade, Cheltenham This fountain and the sculpture of Neptune drawn by sea-horses is one of the features of Cheltenham's celebrated Promenade. It was erected in 1893 and is of Portland stone. Behind is the splendid terrace of houses that are now perhaps the most elegant Municipal Offices in Britain. Built in 1823-25 they were part of the grand development of the Imperial Promenade and were then separate town-houses known as Harward's Buildings. Not long after it was completed the terrace was described as being 'after the fashion of the Louvre' and David Verey in the Pevsner series sees it 'as equal to any in Europe'. It is not, however, built of Cotswold stone or even faced with it. By the time it was built, ashlar facing had become too expensive and stucco-faced brick was substituted – coated with 'Roman cement' to give it an authentic limestone look.

Right:
Pittville Pump Room, Cheltenham Cheltenham grew from a tiny village at the bottom of the Cotswold escarpment to a substantial city in the course of about 30 years – roughly from 1800 to 1830. As the years covered the Regency period when English domestic architecture was at its most elegant and affluence among the upper classes had never been higher, the result was a city that for its style and grace has few equals in Europe. Two geological factors contributed to Cheltenham's progress, both of them Cotswold in origin. The first was the Cotswold waters that having percolated through the oolite, flow through the Lower Lias at the bottom of the Jurassic limestone stack and bubble up, some rich in mineral salts, under the sandy outcrop on which Cheltenham stands. The second was the Inferior Oolite freestone that was so readily available on the face of the escarpment at Leckhampton Hill – so easily quarried in fact that it could be offered in 1810 at 1d a ton, delivered. Another factor was royal patronage. A single visit by the ailing George III in 1788 was enough to put Cheltenham on the map of an aristocratic society that was beginning to be bored by increasingly bourgeois Bath. By 1814 the number of wells had risen to over 30 and by the time this Pump Room was completed in 1830 by John Forbes for Joseph Pitt, to over 50. The style is Greek Revival and based on an engraving of the Temple of Illissus in Athens and it is surrounded by a magnificent garden and the elegant Pittville estate – truly *rus in urbe*. 'Taking the waters' was merely the focus for other activities and this Pump Room has a ball room and facilities for cards, billiards, and the like. Despite its elegance and attraction, the Pittville enterprise was not a financial success and Joseph Pitt died deeply in debt in 1842. The Pump Room and gardens were bought by the Cheltenham Corporation in 1890.

Right:
Sezincote, near Bourton-on-the-Hill Sir Charles Cockerell was a 'nabob' – he had made a fortune in the service of the East India Company and when he returned home he built this house c1805. It was the first Indian style building in England and set something of a fashion. His brother, S. P. Cockerell, was an accomplished architect and he had already built one house in the Indian style for the arch-nabob Warren Hastings at Daylesford before the latter's impeachment. The Cockerell brothers also had the help of an expert on Indian architecture and landscaping in Thomas Daniell and the flair of Humphrey Repton, the landscape gardener. The result is an Indian exterior housing a Classical interior built of local stone, but stone that had been dyed to give it an authentic Indian tone. It could be described as the ultimate in the 'Picturesque' movement with its 'Arcadian' setting not coming from Ancient Greece but from even older Ancient India. The movement was at its height during the Regency and there is a close relationship between Sezincote and the Prince Regent's Brighton Pavilion built in 1815, the Prince Regent having been a guest here earlier. Sezincote remains in private hands but the house and gardens are open to the public in the summer months.

Right:
St Peter's, Winchcombe St Peter's is one of the great Cotswold 'wool-churches' and it was rebuilt in the Perpendicular style c1465. The chancel was built at the personal expense of the abbot and the nave and west tower were the responsibility of the parish which had the help of Sir Ralph Boteler, the builder of Sudeley Castle. No doubt many of the wealthy local clothiers also contributed over the years as they did at Campden. One of them may have been John Smallwood, a clothier who manufactured Winchcombe jerseys, famous in their day, and employed more than 500 men doing it. A friend of Henry VII and his queen, Catherine of Aragon, he is said to have led his own band of armed men at the battle of Flodden in 1513. Winchcombe Abbey was dissolved in 1539 and given by Henry VIII to Lord Seymour of Sudeley who totally demolished it. Virtually no trace remains today apart from a door from the abbey in the church with the initials of one of its last abbots. After the Dissolution, the people of Winchcombe fell on hard times and took to growing tobacco. They were successful at this until 1653 when it was stopped by Act of Parliament because it interfered with the trade from Virginia. St Peter's has all the usual Perpendicular attributes of a church of this date although by the standards of Campden, Northleach and Chichester, the tower and porch are somewhat restrained.

Previous page:
St James's Church, Chipping Campden One of the great wool churches of the Cotswolds, St James's is believed to have been rebuilt in the Perpendicular style by the same masons who built the church at Northleach (p58). There was a Norman church here and it was rebuilt in the 13th and 14th centuries. The Perpendicular transformation included rebuilding the nave arcades and clerestory and began c1450 and finished with the elaborately decorated west tower about the end of the 15th century. Records do not reveal who paid for the work but two wool merchants, both buried in the church, William Welley (d1450) and John Bradway (d1488) left money in their wills for it. To the right of the church are the twin lodges of the old Campden Manor built by Sir Baptist Hicks c1613. The house itself was occupied by the Royalists early in the Civil War when the garrison was called to join the King and march to the relief of Chester. And 'lest the enemy should make use of the house for garrison when he left it' the commander, Sir Henry Bard, was ordered by Prince Rupert to burn the house to the ground. Only one wall of the house survives but two pavilions and an almonry are almost intact.

Right:
The Gatehouse, Stanway Here are the 'rounded gables and Renaissance gateways' that Massingham thought betrayed the Cotswold style. But does it? It is in the best of yellow Guiting stone and was built about 1630. We still have gables, labels, lintels and lights. The verticality is Elizabethan Perpendicular, the bay windows are Gothic and so are the finials on the gables. The shape of the gables is Dutch and the chimney stacks and the gateway surround are Classical – not a very great departure for Tudor Gothic. Moreover, the quality of the mason craft is superb from the ashlared stonework to the masterly carving of the decorative detail. Its quality of design and execution is such that for many years it was even accredited to Inigo Jones, perhaps the greatest of English architects who brought the Classical style to Britain but made it English in the process. In fact it was probably built by Timothy Strong, a Cotswold master-mason. The manor of Stanway belonged to the Abbot of Tewkesbury for about 800 years and was acquired by the Tracy family after the Dissolution. They built the manor house in Elizabethan and Jacobean times and part of it is visible on the right standing at right angles to the gatehouse. It is still in the hands of descendants of the Tracy family and it and its gardens and arboretum are open to the public at times during the summer months.

S
N
SACRED
TO THE MEMORY OF
AND ANNIE HARDING
JOHN ROBERTS HARDING
WILLIAM
AND ANNIE HARDING
WILLIAM HARDING
RICHARD TAYLOR
ELIZABETH

Left:
St Peter & St Paul, Northleach 'Pray for ye children of Thomas Fortey . . .' says a brass in Northleach church on a wool merchant who died in 1447 and was, the brass tells us, a 'renovator of roads and churches'. Nearby another brass remembers his son, John Fortey who died in 1459. His feet rest on a woolsack, his trade mark and his initials are in wreathed medallions around the border. We know that he was responsible for adding the clerestory to the nave including the great nine-light windows visible here above the east windows of the chancel. He and his father are also thought to have been involved in the construction of the nave itself. This is perhaps the most gracious of the great Cotswold wool churches, earlier and less elaborate than Chipping Campden, Cirencester or Fairford. Massingham says of it 'beauty is still a spirit' not a testimony of wealth . . . The other wool-churches of the Cotswolds look more like handsome bribes to heaven.' It is of local stone, a grey-gold Great Oolite rather than the yellower Inferior Oolite of Campden and Winchcombe. The pinnacled structure on the south (left) side of the church is the two-storey porch similar to the one at Burford, but despite the fact that it is 'image-ridden' it escaped the Puritan vandals of the Civil War period but its sculptures are now badly weathered.

Right:
Dutton Almshouses, Northleach Northleach was founded as a new market town in 1227 by the Abbot of Gloucester who gave up 50 acres of his manor at Eastington for the purpose. For the first three centuries of its existence it thrived on the wool trade but when water-powered mechanisation came in during the early Tudor period, the little River Leach was not powerful enough to drive machinery and the trade departed to the Frome valley. Early in the 17th century the lord of the manor, William Dutton, left his manor house and £200 to help the unemployed hoping that the revenue would provide for 'some honest tradesman in freestanes (freestone) or stuffs or in any other such trade as may keep the people from idleness'. In 1616 Dutton's brother, Thomas, built these almshouses. As might be expected from their date, they have all the attributes of traditional Cotswold domestic style – gables with verges and finials, mullioned windows with drip moulds which are continuous on the ground floor, lintels and lights. The doorways have four-centred arches and Dutton's initials appear in the spandrel of the centre one. Northleach itself recovered when it became a staging post on the turnpike road across the Cotswolds in the 17th century and 18th century only to decline again when the railway passed it by. Now with the busy A40 passing through it, it is the modern equivalent of a staging post.

Right:
Arlington Row, Bibury William Morris's enthusiasm for the Cotswolds in general and Bibury in particular extended also to its vernacular architecture. This row of cottages met all his romantic aspirations — built of local stone, crafted by local masons in a style whose origins went back to medieval monastic building. One source records that they were the subject of a painting by C. A. Leslie which achieved particular acclaim at the Royal Academy in 1898. In this regard they have been one of the Cotswold's landmarks ever since, woods in the background and water-meadows and the river in front — the Picturesque so expensively sought after by the builders of great country houses in the 18th century and achieved here by happy accident on a vernacular scale. They are among the most photographed buildings in Britain but their style and history justifies their inclusion here. A row of cottages occupied by weavers who supplied wool for fulling to the local streamside mill, they probably date from the early 17th century. There is evidence that they were adapted from an earlier more open building possibly timber-framed. Two points of interest — one is the absence of drip moulds and the other the way in which the stone slates project over some of the gables — like stone bonnets — without the usual coping stones. The cottages have been owned by the National Trust since 1949 but are not open to the public.

Right:
Bibury Court, Bibury As it winds its way from its steep-sided valley near Yarnworth, the Coln passes through a necklace of sparkling lapidary villages, some carrying the river's own name — Coln St Denis, Coln Rogers, Winson, Ablington, Bibury, Coln St Aldwyns — then past Fairford to join the Thames above Lechlade. That Bibury has become the best known is due to a large extent to the 'discovery' of the village by William Morris, the Victorian artist and 'arts and crafts' romantic in 1871 when he moved into Kelmscott Manor about 12 miles away. He described it as 'lying down in the winding valley besides the clear Coln' as 'surely the most beautiful village in England'. And where Morris with his love of craftsmanship and all things medieval trod on his frequent walks, thousands have followed on foot, on bicycles but nowadays, in cars. Surprisingly Bibury has retained its beauty. One of its attractions is this superb Jacobean house, now an hotel. Originally a Tudor house it was enlarged in 1633 by Sir Thomas Sackville and besides its usual Tudor gables and string-courses, it has a Dutch gable and a main doorway with Classical columns. The Sackville arms and the date are over the door.

Overleaf:
Chavenage House, Tetbury After the Dissolution of the Monasteries the manor of Horsley, which included a small priory, was granted to Sir Edward Seymour. In about 1564 it was bought by the Stephens family and this house was probably built about that date. It is E-shaped and rejoices in the traditional Cotswold Tudor Gothic style although some of the latter may well have come from an earlier house. There is also a wealth of heraldic stained glass. The Stephens were moderate Parliamentarians during the Civil War and, in 1648, Cromwell and his deputy, Ireton, visited Chavenage to persuade Col Stephens to sign the Bill of Impeachment which led to Charles I's trial and subsequent execution. At first reluctant, Stephens eventually agreed and, legend has it, thereby brought down a curse on the house. Any Lord of the Manor dying in the house is carried away in a black coach driven by a headless horseman clad in the robes of the Order of the Garter — King Charles himself, no less. The Stephens, once prosperous wool farmers fell on hard times and Chavenage was bought in 1894 by the Lowsley-Williams family who still own it. It is open to the public during the summer months.

Left:
Painswick Churchyard Painswick's churchyard is justifiably famous. An authority on Cotswold churches, David Verey, suggests it 'must be about the best in England'. One feature is its celebrated yews — some say 99 of them, others 105 — planted in 1792 and clipped and shaped like architectural finials ever since. Another is its remarkable collection of table tombs mostly of the 17th and 18th centuries. These are frequently found in Cotswold churchyards and in many cases are as much a product of the wealth generated by the wool trade as are wool-churches. Some early ones are known as 'bale-tombs' because they resemble bales of wool. The ones seen here are of two types — the 'tea-caddies', tallish, octagonal or cylindrical with distinctive lids: there is a fine specimen in the middleground — and late 18th century in date. The other type has lyre-shaped ends — there are two on the left — and are usually earlier, reflecting the Dutch influences at the end of the 17th century. Most of the tombs are heavily decorated with Classical motifs in the Baroque and Rococo style and are examples of masonic craftsmanship of the highest order. Many are the work of a well-known Painswick family of masons and carvers who were active throughout the 18th century, the Bryans. Many have been restored recently.

4
Avon & Wiltshire

Right:
Malmesbury Abbey Standing high on a hill above the Avon, Malmesbury was the site of one of the most celebrated Saxon abbeys founded in the 7th century by St Aldhelm. The abbey was rebuilt by the Normans c1160 and again in the 14th century. At the Dissolution it was granted to a wealthy clothier, William Stumpe, who gave the nave of the church to the parish and used the other monastic buildings for cloth manufacture. During the 17th century the west tower fell down and other buildings became ruinous. The nave was walled off when the tower fell and the gap in the clerestory is quite evident. But the masterpiece of masoncraft is the great south doorway, one of the best examples of Norman sculpture in Britain. Although they are now rather defaced, the eight orders — the successive inner arches — that make up the porch are carved with beaded patterns some of which have figure sculptures that tell the Old Testament story from the Creation to David and Goliath. A possible date for the sculpture has been suggested as c1170. Malmesbury and the story of 'Oliver the Monk' are dear to the hearts of all airmen because in c1003 — 900 years before the Wright brothers — he made himself wings and flew off the top of abbey tower and though crippled by his heavy landing, at least lived to tell the first ever pilot's tale. Abbey roofs seem to have an attraction to flyers — see Lacock (p73).

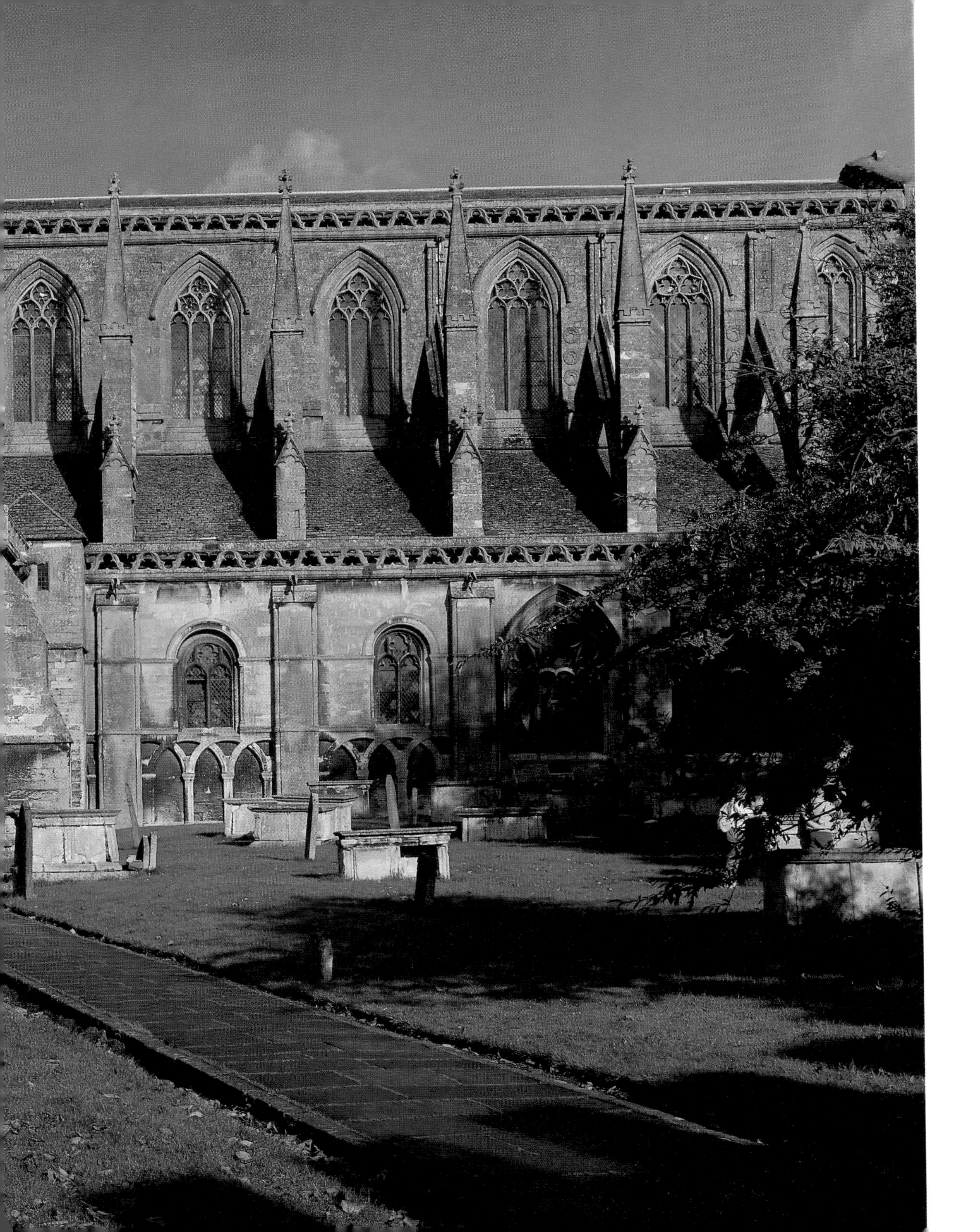

Right:
Charlton Park House What is usually known as a 'prodigy' house, Charlton Park House was built c1610 for the Countess of Suffolk, wife of the first Earl of Suffolk who had built the much bigger Audley End in Suffolk a decade earlier. Queen Elizabeth was given to making 'progresses' each summer, moving from one major courtier's house to another accompanied by a large retinue. She was highly critical of the accommodation and entertainment she was afforded and Heaven help any lordling who failed to please her. To curry royal favour — and reap the subsequent rewards of office — her noble courtiers vied with each other in building, at vast expense, houses that were not only fitting for the entertainment of royalty but also gave expression to the builder's taste and personality. The aim was to impress and what Vanbrugh was a century later to call the 'castle air' — towers and ogee caps and 'busie' skylines — is usually evident. The trend continued into the reign of James I and there are numerous 'prodigy houses' throughout the country — Audley End, Woolaton Hall and Hardwick being the best known examples, but Charlton is the only one in the Cotswold stone area. It is of local stone and, one might say, has gables and labels, lintels and lights writ large. 'Fantastical' is another word often used about such houses. Neither house did the Earl and Countess much good. He fell from grace in 1618 and though rehabilitated later he never achieved the high office needed to recoup his investment. The house was altered c1770 and the interior is mainly Georgian. It is still owned by the family and is open to the public in the summer months.

Left:
Lydiard Mansion, Lydiard Tregoze Whereas many manor houses and churches in the Cotswold area have a village around them, here at Lydiard Tregoze there is a house and a church but no village. The name means a site near a hill and 'Tregoze' is a corruption of the name of the Norman family who owned the manor, Troisgots. The estate belonged to the St John family from the 15th to the 20th century and the church has served mainly as their family chapel. A medieval house on the site was remodelled in 1743 for the second Viscount St John and is of the early Palladian Classical style which began to replace Baroque in the 1730s. It is very similar to the much earlier south front of Wilton House which has been attributed to Inigo Jones, the inspiration of the English Palladian school. The architect of Lydiard is believed to have been Roger Morris (d1749) who also designed the Palladian Bridge at Wilton. The church behind the house is notable for its rich furnishings and in particular for its monuments. These include one dated 1592 of Nicholas St John and his wife kneeling side by side in Elizabethan dress. Lydiard Mansion was bought by Swindon Corporation in 1943 (now the Borough of Thamesdown) and is used as a conference centre but is open to the public throughout the year.

Above:
Lacock Abbey, near Chippenham The abbey was founded in 1232 by Ela, Countess of Salisbury in memory of her husband, William Longespee, one of the knights who witnessed the signing of the Magna Carta in 1215. Completed about 1247, it was built of Great Oolite specially quarried at Hazlebury near Box, and Ela became its first abbess. It was dissolved in 1539 and granted by Henry VIII to Sir William Sharington who demolished the church, leaving only the north wall, and adapted the rest as his house. He also built a Stable Court to the north and an octagonal tower in the former chancel. Much of the ground storey of the abbey has, however, survived unaltered and constitutes the most extensive medieval nunnery buildings in the country. Sharington's successors were the Talbot family who lived in the Abbey until 1958. Legend has it that Olive Sharington in 1574 leapt off the abbey roof because her parents refused to let her marry John Talbot. Her long skirts, it is said, billowed out and slowed her fall so that Talbot standing below was able to catch her. (After that he *had* to marry her!) In 1754-56 John Ivory Talbot remodelled the west range seen here — in the middle is the hall with its tall ogee-headed windows, its turrets, its pinnacles and its pierced parapet. It was designed by Sanderson Miller (d1780) in the Gothic fashion of the day. To the right is the dining room and round the corner behind the cedar tree is the old north wall of the church. Just visible on the wall are the two Gothic oriel windows put in by William Henry Fox Talbot in 1830. In 1835 he took the first photographic negative ever made which featured one of them. The abbey was given to the National Trust in 1944 and is open to the public in the summer months.

Far left:
St Nicholas' Church, Hardenhuish, Chippenham Pronounced 'Harnish', this Scottish-sounding name is Old English probably meaning a 'huish' or family holding on high ground — the limestone hillside above Chippenham. This small Georgian church is one of only two in the whole of Wiltshire — the other is at Wardour Castle — and probably the only one in the Cotswolds. It is ashlar-faced in Cotswold stone and was built to a design by one of Bath's great architects, John Wood the younger, in 1779 although his plans were not entirely followed — the west tower is an addition. In the churchyard a point of interest is the canopied tomb of David Ricardo the celebrated writer on economic matters and an early advocate of monetarism. The son of a Dutch Jew, he made a fortune on the London Stock Exchange which enabled him to retire at the age of 42 and devote his time to writing his *Principles of Political Economy and Taxation* published in 1817. In 1813 he bought the now royal estate of Gatcombe Park just across the border in Gloucestershire and died — of an ear infection — in 1823, aged 51. Economics were not his only interest. He founded the Geological Society and his tomb is crowned by a Corinthian column and four nearly-nude maidens.

Left:
Methuen Folley, Corsham At this point in the book, readers will no doubt recognise the stone, but what about the style? Is it a castle or yet more abbey ruins? The answer is that it was probably built in 1844-49 for Lord Methuen of Corsham Court by the architect Thomas Bellamy, possibly to disguise the stables, certainly to impart an ecclesiastical rather than a 'castle' air. It used stones and tracery from Chippenham Abbey. Solidly and carefully built it is a true 'folly' but hardly one that could be called Picturesque.

Right:
Corsham Court As the sun catches the stone of the south front, the older lichened Cotswold limestone can be seen peeping behind the newer cleaner stone, the Elizabethan Gothic from behind the Victorian Classical. Corsham Court was first built about 1580 for Thomas Smythe, a London haberdasher and Collector of Customs. In 1745, Paul Methuen whose family had made a fortune in the wool industry bought the house in anticipation of a legacy of a superb collection of pictures and other *objets d'arts* he was to receive from his uncle, Sir Paul Methuen, a diplomat with long service abroad. He received his inheritance in 1757 and soon afterwards began work on converting the house into a display gallery for the collection. Thereafter the architectural history of the house is largely related to successive remodellings to house the steadily expanding collection. The first, in 1761, was carried out by Lancelot 'Capability' Brown (d1783) who widened the two Elizabethan wings on the south front but kept their style and changed the east range into a picture gallery. In 1800, John Nash (d1835) the great London town-planner, enlarged the house again by building on a north wing. He also added the buttress turrets. About 1845, Thomas Bellamy pulled down Nash's work and built a square middle section with a monumental staircase. He also added the rather heavy-handed Jacobean exterior work — transomed bays and pediments with what Vanbrugh might have called 'eminences'. The house is still in the hands of the Methuen family and together with its collection is open to the public at selected times of the year.

Right:
Hungerford School and Almshouses, Corsham Corsham was an estate village and has a wealth of houses, large and small and of a variety of styles mostly built of the local stone which continues to be mined rather than quarried at Monks Park. Between the first Elizabethan owner of Corsham Court and the arrival of the Methuens, it was owned by the Hungerfords and the Thynnes. The Hungerfords built this school and a range of almshouses to the north of it in 1668 and it is an almost perfect example of the Cotswold vernacular with neo-Classical Jacobean overtones. There are gables and labels and the schoolroom windows on the right of the porch are pure Gothic. The porch with its pediment, its elaborately carved coat of arms and what looks like an attempt at a Venetian window on the side is early English Baroque.

Right:
Sheldon Manor, Chippenham There was once a village here and in the manner of Cotswold villages, presumably a church; now only the manor survives with a small detached 15th century chapel. And, judging by the size of its surviving doorway the earlier manor house — dating from 1282 — must have been much bigger than the present house. It mostly dates from the 17th century when shortly after the Civil War most of the ruined old house was demolished and a new one built. Since that time the house has had a chequered history and was at one time divided into two farmhouses but has nonetheless been continuously lived in for over 700 years . . . Like many old houses it is said to have a ghost, indeed not one ghost but several. Inside the old porch is a drinking trough fed by a pipe from the roof and on stormy nights a group of horsemen has been seen to ride up to the house and water its horses. Who are they — or more correctly, who were they? Nobody now living knows, but legend has it that they are Royalist soldiers who nearly fought a battle with the Roundheads at Chippenham in 1643 but both sides thought better of it and rode away. The house has been in the hands of the Gibbs family in recent times and is open to the public during the summer months.

Right:
Horton Court, Chipping Sodbury The Cotswold vernacular again and this time with Norman origins. On the far left is the church built in the 14th century on a Norman site. Immediately next to it and wearing a scarlet veil of Virginia Creeper is the single-storey Norman 'great hall', c1140, the remains of a prebendal or priest's house. It is now the north wing of the manor house. Clearly visible is the Norman chevron moulding round the doorway. After various alterations over the centuries, the great hall was restored as nearly as possible to its original state in 1860. The rest of the house was built in 1521 for William Knight who in 1527 as Bishop of Bath and Wells went to Rome to attempt to obtain a divorce for Henry VIII from Catherine of Aragon. When Horton was built, Knight was a 'protonotary' — a recorder of the court — and the Renaissance surround to the main door has carvings of his official hat and his coat of arms. He also built an ambulatory — a type of cloister — in the Perpendicular style with early Renaissance features in the garden. The house was over-restored in 1927. It is now owned by the National Trust and the hall and ambulatory are open to the public in the summer months.

Right:
Dyrham Park The park sits under the edge of the southwest escarpment near the place where the Saxons in 577 defeated the Britons, killed three kings and moved on to capture Gloucester, Cirencester and Bath. The name Dyrham can mean two things — to the Saxons, a deer park; to the Britons they defeated, a place of water in the form of numerous springs. And both could be true. Fallow deer have roamed the estate for centuries and in the early days of the house there was a canal, a cascade and fountains. It was built in 1692 by William Blaithwayt who was Secretary of State for War to William III who first employed a Huguenot architect, Samuel Hauduroy. Later, in 1698, he was able to call on the services of William Talman, one of the royal architects who worked under Wren. Talman designed this east front in what is in effect a second house back to back with the earlier one. The stone came from Tolldown quarry about a mile away and the style is English Baroque but in the restrained manner of Wren rather than the flamboyance of Vanbrugh and Hawksmoor at Blenheim Palace. Talman was involved with the building of Wren's Hampton Court Palace and designed Chatsworth to which Dyrham has been likened. The house, its contents and the garden were bought from the Blaithwayt family in 1956 by the Ministry of Works, and the estate in 1976. Both were transferred to the National Trust and the house is open to the public in the summer months.

Right:
Iford Manor, Bradford-on-Avon The river here is the Frome — just to confuse matters, not the Golden Valley Frome but a tributary of the Avon rather than the Severn. Like Avon and Stour, 'Frome' is a Welsh river name frequently found but this time meaning fresh, vigorous, even sparkling. The bridge is medieval, c1400, the house Tudor and the statue of Britannia on the bridge is early 20th century. The house was refronted in ashlared Bath stone in the Classical style — balustrading, pediments over the windows — c1725-30 and was once a centre of the local cloth industry. It was bought in 1899 by Harold A. Peto, a Victorian landscape gardener who refurbished the garden with Classical statuary and ornamentation, including a cloister and many rare plants, in a manner that would have delighted the heart of 18th century lovers of the Picturesque. The gardens are open to the public at times during the summer months.

Right:
Claverton Manor, Bath Ralph Allan the supplier of stone for the building of Bath owned the older manor house at Claverton and although he later built Prior Park, chose to be buried in the churchyard here high above the Avon valley. The present manor house was built c1820 and the architect was Jeffrey Wyatt (d1840) who is famous for the remodelling of Windsor Castle for George IV between 1824-30 when he added 'ville' to his name and was knighted. Generally known as a specialist in neo-Gothic and Tudor-revival buildings, Wyatt adopted pure Palladian Classicism for his design of the west front of Claverton — two and a half storeys high, rusticated basement, centre pediment supported by giant Ionic pilasters, under a parapeted hipped roof, it was elegant if somewhat old-fashioned for its Regency date. The south front has two large segmental bow windows, rather more in keeping with the times. Now owned by the American Museum in Britain, Claverton has furnished period rooms and galleries of textiles, pewter, glass and silver to illustrate the background of American domestic life between the 17th and 19th centuries. It also has American gardens and an American arboretum and is open to the public in the summer months.

Left:
Abbey Churchyard, Bath On the surface, Bath is sited in a vast amphitheatre surrounded by cliff-like Jurassic limestone hills with the wide valley of the Avon on three sides. Deep underground, however, older rocks have formed a deep bowl or syncline, one rim of which emerges through the surface as the Mendip Hills. Rainwater falling on the Mendips thousands of years ago has seeped down through the rocks that make up the bowl and has been heated by the earth's central core. Under pressure it has been forced up the other side of the bowl to emerge from a fault under Bath in three hot springs with temperatures of about 45°C — that of a pleasant bath. The Romans liked bathing and built bath-houses and temples around the springs. The Saxons didn't believe in bathing and destroyed the city in 577 and the ruins lay buried until c1880. The Normans didn't bath much but the monks knew a good site when they saw one and built an abbey with a great cathedral church in the 12th century. By 1499, the cathedral was in ruins and the monks displayed all the laxities, moral as well as religious, that were later to lead to the Dissolution. In that year a new Bishop of Bath and Wells (Oliver King) who was also Abbot of Bath, laid about him and tightened discipline. In particular he had the abbey church rebuilt in the prevailing Perpendicular style using the King's masons, the Vertue brothers, who also built Henry VII's chapel in Westminster Abbey and St George's Chapel at Windsor. (The work was not completed until 1869.) The west front seen here resembles that at Windsor but has much more elaborate carving. The sculptures are of angels climbing up and down ladders to Heaven, those coming down doing it head first. Next to the abbey west front is a temple of a different era — the Classical frontage of the entry to the Roman Baths completed in 1897.

Right:
The Circus, Bath The Circus — or the King's Circus as it was originally called — is both John Wood the Elder's masterpiece and his memorial. He intended it to be a large circular open space with three streets running into it and dividing a great circle of three-tiered buildings into separate sweeping arcs. The idea is said to have been inspired by the Coliseum in Rome. The buildings are all of Bath stone — no Roman cement-faced brick as at Cheltenham. The embellishment is pure Classical architecture at its best — each tier carrying engaged pillars of a different order from Doric up to Corinthian. Wood completed the design in the year of his death but his son completed the work in 1758. The open space effect intended by Wood was unfortunately lost when trees were planted in the Circus in 1790. Bath, however, is not short of open spaces and one of them, the Royal Victoria Park created in 1830, is alight with glorious colour from March to December with a glimpse through the trees to the glinting stone of the Royal Crescent. And finally, as Massingham put it, 'Bath . . . is the magnificently formal tailpiece to the end of a chapter' — the Cotswold's southern full-stop.

Right:
Pulteney Bridge, Bath Although sick and crippled people had been seeking relief from its hot springs since the middle of the 17th century, Bath's recognition as a watering place for royalty and the aristocracy did not come until the 18th century. It was then that Bath's 'great rebuilding' began. The instigator was the gamester, Richard 'Beau' Nash, who developed Bath as an elegant 18th century Monte Carlo and dominated the city for over half a century. The architect and planner of the expansion on to the surrounding hills was John Wood the Elder (d1754), no mean entrepreneur himself, and helped by the supplier of the Bath stone, Ralph Allan. He was followed by his son John Wood the Younger (d1781) who built the Royal Crescent (p93). Sir John Pulteney owned the Bathwick estate on the east side of the Avon and in 1769 built this bridge to facilitate its development. The architect was Robert Adam (d1792), perhaps the greatest architect of the 18th century. It is Palladian in style and has Adam's favourite motif of a triumphal arch in the centre of the superstructure. Like the Ponte Vecchio in Florence it is flanked with shops on both sides. It was mutilated by the Victorians but was carefully restored in 1976 by the Georgian Group.

Bibliography

General

The Pattern of English Building; Alec Clifton-Taylor; Faber, 1980.
Houses in the Landscape; John & Jane Penoyre; Faber, 1978.
The National Trust Guide; R. Fedden & R. Joekes; Cape, 1973.
Folklore, Myths and Legends of Britain; Readers' Digest, 1973.
British Building Styles Recognition; Alan Hollingsworth; Ian Allan Ltd, 1987.
Historic House, Castles and Gardens Open to the Public; Leisure Publications, 1988.
English Stone Building; Alec Clifton-Taylor & A. S. Ireson; Gollancz, 1983.
The Smaller English House; Lyndon F. Cave; Hale, 1981.
Parish Churches; Hugh Braun; Faber, 1974.
Vernacular Architecture; Journal of the Vernacular Architecture Group, 1981-88, *passim.*
Architectural History; Journal of the Society of Architectural Historians of Great Britain, 1981-88, *passim.*
A Guide to the Abbeys of England & Wales; Anthony New; Constable, 1985.

Cotswolds

Cotswolds Churches; David Verey; Batsford, 1976.
Cotswold Country; H. J. Massingham; Batsford, 1937.
Portrait of the Cotswolds; Edith Brill; Hale, 1977.
Geology Explained in the Severn Vale & Cotswolds; William Dreghorn; David and Charles, 1967.
The Gloucestershire Landscape; H. P. R. Finberg; Hodder & Stoughton, 1975.
The Buildings of England; ed Nikolaus Pevsner; Penguin Books:
Gloucestershire: The Cotswolds; David Verey, 1974.
Gloucestershire: The Vale & The Forest of Dean; David Verey, 1980.
Warwickshire; N. Pevsner & Alexandra Wedgwood, 1966.
Oxfordshire; N. Pevsner & Jennifer Sherwood, 1979.
Wiltshire; N. Pevsner, revised Bridget Cherry, 1981.
Worcestershire; N. Pevsner, 1977.
The Folklore of the Cotswolds; K. M. Briggs; Batsford, 1974.
Old Cottages & C in the Cotswold District; E. Guy Dawber & W. G. Davie; Batsford, 1905.
Along the Cotswold Ways; G. R. Crosher; Pan, 1976.
Highways and Byways in Oxford and the Cotswolds; Herbert Evans; MacMillan, 1905.

Index

Page

Aston-sub-Edge, Manor Farm, Wilts — 13
Bath, Avon – The Circus — 93
Bath, Avon – Abbey Churchyard — 90
Bath, Avon-Pulteney Bridge — 94
Bibury, Glos – Arlington Row — 63
Bibury, Glos – Bibury Court — 65
Blenheim Palace — 30
Blenheim Palace, Oxon – Great Court — 33
Blenheim Palace, Oxon – Water Garden — 35
Bloxham Church, Oxon — 42
Bradford-on-Avon – Iford Manor — 87
Bradford-on-Avon, Wilts – Saxon Church — 6
Bradford-on-Avon, Wilts – Westbury House — 15
Broadway, Worcs – St Eadburgh's — 47
Broughton Castle, Oxon — 41
Burford, Oxon – Church — 28
Charlton Park House, Wilts — 71
Chastleton House, Oxon — 39
Chavenage, Glos — 66
Cheltenham, Glos – Pittville Pump Room — 51
Cheltenham, Glos – The Promenade — 49
Chipping Campden – Almshouses — 16
Chipping Campden, Glos – Church — 55
Claverton Manor, Avon — 89
Corsham Court, Wilts — 77
Corsham Folly — 75
Corsham School, Wilts — 79
Duntisbourne Rouse, Glos — 9

Page

Dyrham Park, Avon — 85
Evesham, Worcs – Almonry — 45
Evesham, Worcs – Bell Tower — 43
Fairford Church, Glos — 3
Great Chalfield Manor, Wilts — 10
Great Coxwell Barn, Oxon — 29
Hailes Abbey, Glos — 4
Hardenhuish Church, Wilts — 74
Horton Court, Avon — 83
Lacock Abbey, Wilts — 73
Lydiard Mansion, Wilts — 72
Malmesbury, Wilts – Abbey — 69
Minster Lovell Hall, Oxon — 25
Northleach, Glos – Almshouses — 61
Northleach, – St Peter & St Paul — 58
Oxford – Christ Church — 20
Oxford – Magdalen College — 23
Oxford – Old School Quad — 22
Oxford – Radcliffe Camera — 21
Oxford – Tom Tower — 20
Oxford from Boar's Hill — 19
Painswick – Churchyard — 67
Rousham House, Oxon — 37
Sezincote, Glos — 53
Sheldon Manor, Wilts — 81
Shipton Court, Oxon — 27
Stanway Gatehouse — 57
Winchcombe, St Peters — 54